MORPHEUS DIPS HIS OAR

MORPHEUS DIPS HIS OAR

poems

Tamara Madison

Sheila-Na-Gig Editions

Morpheus Dips His Oar Copyright © 2023 Tamara Madison
Cover photo: Tamara Madison
Author photo: Sharon De La O

ISBN: 9798987305829
Library of Congress Control Number: 2023932885

Published by Sheila-Na-Gig Editions
Russell, KY
Hayley Mitchell Haugen, Editor
www.sheilanagigblog.com

Acknowledgments

Along the Fault Line (Picture Show Press, 2022): "Ace"

Braided Way: "To a Grieving Friend"

Chiron Review: "Flesh Remembers," "The Nicest Man"

Cholla Needles: "Night Journey," "The Stories of My Dreams"

Gatherings, an art and poetry-based experiment in giving and receiving: "Quarantine Spring"

Poemeleon: "Blue Nude"

Rat's Ass Review: "Black Cadillac," "The Tyranny of Photographs"

Rise Up Review: "Assisted Living Singalong"

Sheila-Na-Gig online: "Fire Sky," "The Great Sea," "Iodine," "Orchid Cactus"

Shot Glass Journal: "Fugue," "Nature's Revenge" (as "The Labor It Takes")

Shrewlitmag: "When the Mind Unwinds"

Steve Kowit Poetry Prize: "Waiting for the Scythe" (Honorable Mention)

The Belly Remembers (Chapbook Winner, Jane Buel Bradley Poetry Prize, Pearl Editions, 2004): "Seeing Paris"

Worcester Review: "Earth's Mercy"

Your Daily Poem: "Mothers," "The Guys Who Work Inside My Head"

For a time,
I rest in the grace of the world, and am free—
—Wendell Berry

Contents

I. Cultivated Secrets

II. Sacraments

III. Water Rising

I.

Cultivated Secrets

The Great Sea

A Buddhist once said each life
is a river branching off a larger river,
and every river flows in its own path
to the great sea that is death.
I imagine my parents in that sea—
his bear-arms pulling side stroke,
pale legs scissoring the green tide,
her in a flowered swim cap doing
an Esther Williams churn—
one stroke face down, one stroke up.
I doubt they've even looked
for one another there; now, each one
visits me. Even on this chilly morning
I feel the circles of their separate
embraces, hers close—I can almost
feel her spirit-breath—his wide
as a ring of Saturn. Now
they've swum off far into that sea;
may it keep them ever cycling
on its currents back to me.

Mothers

Tonight as the moon draws its arc
through the stars and fog thickens
on the bay, a hummingbird
sits on her nest in the fuchsia plant

warming her one almond-shaped egg.
My adult children, home for a holiday,
strum guitars in the living room
and I wonder how many other mothers

are here on this little plot of land: possum,
mouse, raccoon? There must be spider
mothers here, too, and mother worms.
But I've seen this hummingbird, how

she sits on her nest as though in a boat
sailing on the breezes of spring and into
the fogs of night. I remember how I kept
my own offspring warm in my womb

as they turned into babies, and then
became the two adults making music
in their childhood home. Soon the egg
will hatch and a tiny being will emerge,

wet and scrawny, and it will grow
so big that one day the nest will be too small
and Mother will move out, flying back
every half hour to feed the hungry little beak.

My children themselves have moved away;
now they're the ones who must fly back
on holidays, guitars and laundry in hand,
returning to the nest to nourish their mother.

Catching Children

My mother sketched in quick lines overlapping.
Gradually, the subject emerged, like a Polaroid
exposed to light. Most often she drew people,
sometimes children, though they moved so fast—
like fireflies, they had to be caught. Here's
my daughter when her hair was fair in curls
around her face, on a dinner napkin with the word
"caught" and the date. Children not her own,
even grandchildren, were a mystery to Mother,
but she could draw them, stilled like insects
on flypaper, like butterflies pinned to a board
where they would be forever quiet and obey.

Iodine

We howled out against the pain
when Mother rubbed the red wand hard
against our soap-scrubbed wounds.
She tugged our loosening teeth
before they were ready, pulled them
with a yank that echoed in our skulls.
She ripped bandaids off
before we even knew, taking scabs
and arm hairs with them. I feel her
watching from beyond right now
as I try to tell him: *Go, let me live my life!*
But I use Bactine, not iodine, and he's
like one of my children's teeth
that I wouldn't pull until it was
swinging-door loose. Our life together—
a bandaid for loneliness, now frayed.
Pull it off! I hear my mother say.
Still, I wait for the gum to loosen
so I won't have to speak
these stinging words.

Measles

One after the other we fell,
first my brother, then my sister,
then I, the youngest, each one
banished to the living room
to sleep alone on the folding bed
with our fevers and the spots
that burned like campfires.
Mother washed our dishes
separately, came in every hour
with a thermometer dipped
in alcohol, orange juice
with a bendy straw. It seemed
like forever, the heat, the isolation,
the pain, even on our palms,
the loneliness in the high-
ceilinged room where I had spent
so many long summer days
imagining ceiling as floor,
wondering what life would be like
if we walked on stucco
instead of carpet, if furniture hung,
unreachable, from the ceiling,
never imagining how tired
I'd become of this fantasy,
or that by the time I'd have children
of my own one quick prick
would forever deprive them
of this miserable solitude.

The Professor's Daughter

She drew carefully in the margins
of her notes—elaborate vines,
leaves, flowers. She was quiet,
childlike, sad for all things young
and innocent. Her father made a big
deal about us, explained the literary
genres that our movies belonged to,
kissed our hands like a continental
gentleman. I didn't understand
my friend's disgust. He was so
sweet! *He drinks champagne all day*
was all she'd say. Once she was
in the hospital for three days,
swallowed a bottle of sleeping pills,
but it didn't work. When I felt down,
a shower or a walk were all I needed.
If she had told me the truth
about what her father did to her,
I would not have understood.
My own father drank scotch
and hooted like an owl; nothing
to hold against a man.

Eating the Artichoke

When you eat your first artichoke
you are daring and cultured,
a member of an elite
with taste refined enough to savor
the delicate flesh in the recess
of thorny tip and barbed leaf,
patient enough to wade
through the thicket of leaves
picking your way to the prickly choke.
You are not like your forebears
crashing through dry grasses
to come upon the bristling bush
with its towers of thorns,
tearing at the painful flowers
in search of sustenance, anything
to help them remain in this life
and be able to pass down
those stalwart genes that would enable
their progeny thousands of years thence
to pick out a shrink-wrapped
pack of thistles from a grocery shelf
and know already, among other
cultivated secrets, the right way
to cook and eat them.

Baby Vegetables

I pry open the plastic clamshell
of baby arugula, tear into the bag
of baby lettuce, pick the baby carrots
from the market bin and tuck them
into my recyclable supermarket tote
with other baby vegetables.
They will be delicious but still
I will feel like a pedophile
enjoying these sweet young flowers
of God's creation before they have grown
to full size, before they have basked
their intended amount in the sunlight
or slept in their earthen wombs,
before they have drunk their allotted share
of earthly water. Someone else
has cut short these tender lives and we,
my friend, are devouring them
like perverts in a damp garage.
And they taste so good.

Drawer

—UCSB, 1973

A few days after the seduction
he decides to talk to me,
asks me to go to the clinic.
Make sure there is no growth,
he says.

Now I am looking up at the light.
My knees are spread and two women
sit at the foot of my table.
They carry on a lively conversation
as they work. I'm not listening.
I feel the warm light
on my newly-wakened
nether world,
and the women begin
to search inside me
as in a drawer.

I imagine them pulling things out—
bottle caps, old tires, tampons of course,
lipstick tubes, wrappers, leaves,
a shred from Seventeen magazine…
But I'm not so old, I want to protest,
I've barely begun my collection!

You're fine, they tell me
and hand me a prescription
to make me bleed. Outside
it's raining. I sit in French class
staring out at the rows
of eucalyptus dripping
in their ragged bark,
at the stream of bicycles
hissing on the wet path.

I watch him round the corner
as always at this time:
brown bike
beard trimmed
violin tucked under one arm
too old to be a student.

Black Cadillac

My mother taught me not
to hate (*but never date*
a Negro; if you had children,
where would they fit in?).
My brother had to work
on the farm; he
was raised by our father.

I ride to school in the cab
of Dad's pickup, sitting
between them, books
and lunch box at my knee.

At a stop light we land
next to a Cadillac with a black
man behind the wheel.
How did that nigger
get himself a Cadillac? they snicker.

Here is the bruise
my memory has carried
for five decades:

My brother rolling down
the window to spit
on the shiny black hood;
our father chuckling.

The Tyranny of Photographs

My mother kept our childhoods enshrined
in framed collages on her walls. She was there,
too, skinny dark-haired girl with a pair
of baby-faced brothers. But most of the photos
showed us as children, teenagers, young adults,
parents with toddlers.

It's been so long since we were those versions
of ourselves. We recall those times, not
as we would remember them, but as the tyranny
of each photograph insists. And according
to that tyranny we are at our best: smiling,
healthy, surrounded by and full of love.

What the photographs don't show is how
we've struggled for money, marriage, and health,
how my brother and I stand on opposite banks
of our parents' philosophy, how our sister's reality
is gradually losing facts and details.

When Mother died, we divided the collages
among ourselves and our children. Now
our younger faces gaze from where they lean
against the walls, and from my own dresser—
my son's and daughter's childhood selves
preserved in frames, little ants in amber.

When the Mind Unwinds

—for my sister

When the mind unwinds
memories lie in ruins.
The bridges that once
linked thoughts collapse
into a jumble of rotting planks
and broken pilings.

When the mind unwinds
it can only go back and never
forward; this is a time
for unlearning.

Whose house is this? Why
are my things here? Who
is that man who says
he's my husband?

When the mind unwinds
some memories stay lodged
like shrapnel—
your mother's ring
and her impatience,
the house with three palms
where you grew up,
the time in high school
when you parked the car
on the tracks,
daring it all to end.

When the mind unwinds
it goes slick as an 8-ball
and everything new to it
slides right off. But you,
you are still in there, the core

of you bending like a reed
in the storm of it,
bending toward an ending.

Cold Morning

I put on my sister's jacket;
her scent still dwells in the seams.
Again I mourn not her death
but her life, the way
she cloistered her longings
within her faith. I don't
understand that faith
in fables that men pass down.
Those god stories will one day
be like footprints on wind-tossed
dunes. My faith is in the chirp
of the phoebe, the vine's
supple sinew. My faith
is the glad embrace, the hand
outstretched to help, the lips
pressed to a fevered forehead.
My faith is in my sister's jacket,
the weight of her still-warm love.

Hubris

We hear my father's bare feet shuffle
down the night hallway, see his shape—
a ruined edifice—shadow the doorway.
We feel him standing there, a grey form
staring, blank, into the darkness
of our half-sleep. We hear him shuffle
off again, back toward his bedroom,
back toward Mother, drifting
in sleep's brief respite.

When Dad was young he drove the spray rig,
its two arms reaching over rows of flowering citrus
in a shower of chemicals that covered
and soaked him. At sundown he came home.
The house shook to the slam of the door,
his shirt and khakis stained orange, reeking
of the poison that killed insects but left
the perfect fruit to flourish. The smell lingered
on his body for days in spite of nightly showers.

My five-year-old draws Grandpa in shaky lines
to show the tremor. Disease makes a mask
of my father's face; his eyes look out
like windows of a vacant building. Here
was the man who roiled our lives like a raging wind
and left behind this trembling shell.

He appears later at the end of the hallway,
a haze of swirling lights that come on odd occasions
until we beg him to stay away. I never see
his ghost except in my own mirror,
but when I catch the aroma of lemon blossoms
wafting through my world in spring, I sense
the essence of him, the man who put me
in this world, the man who gave me half myself,
the man we sometimes used to wish
we did not know.

The Nicest Man

Near the end, all his fierceness
is gone. Stroke-softened, trembling
from Parkinson's, mind veiled
by dementia, this boulder of a man
whose temper terrorized employees
and family alike, spends his days
hunched before the TV watching
M*A*S*H reruns and the Iran-Contra
hearings (*I've always been a Republican,*
but now I'm not so sure, he tells me).
One morning I find the TV tuned to PBS.
Dad! You're watching Mr. Rogers!
The frightening vehemence back
in his face, he turns to me and growls,
THAT is the NICEST man!

Nature's Revenge

She pushes the boulder of her ten decades
back and forth to the bathroom, bemoans
her glacial pace, the labor it takes
to get up from a chair. I tell her *You've lived*
a long life, Mother, this part is just Nature's
revenge, and we laugh. She has loved life;
life has loved her back. It's this love
that keeps her pushing long past the time
that her mind decided she should go.
She wonders what awaits her in her new
dimension; surely more than this. Today,
she says she doesn't want any food,
even as she opens her mouth to the spoon.

Assisted Living Singalong

I know the songs too; my parents sang them
when I was a kid. I know about the strawberry blond,
the tea for two, tiptoeing through the tulips. I know
all the words to Don't Fence Me In, Sweet Georgia Brown,
Somewhere Over the Rainbow. Today, I watch
the singing faces, old mouths open in song, eyes soft
with memory. These people survived The Great Depression,
World War II. They know sacrifice. They helped
save the world from the devil. Now, fascism has marched
over the threshold of our world, hung its hat on the rack,
taken up the stool near the door. When it comes time
for God Bless America I have to stop singing,
the lump of ash full in my throat, as though all
that certainty of goodness, all that hope, burned
and blew right in. May these sweet sacrificers leave
this blighted world believing that it all worked out.

Waiting for the Scythe

She's got 93 years on that body. It still works,
mostly. It needs a brace on one leg *(Consult
a neurologist next time you slip a disc!)*
but it gets around with the help of a purple walker
with zebra stripes. The brain still works most
of the time, especially with the right
old-memory-trigger.

She's going to donate this body to science:
the 93 year-old heart that hasn't always
done the right thing; the overactive digestive tract;
the eyes that have seen so much with their
20-40 vision; the vocal chords that have told jokes,
sung arias in five languages and spoken with authority
even upon ignorance; the bony hands that painted
all the paintings that hang on her walls.
She's pretty sure the Grim Reaper is on his way.
She's been waiting for him for years now.
What use am I here? Why am I still alive?

She's in bed right now in a purple nightgown,
waiting. I tell her, *If you really want him to come,
play hard to get! If you keep throwing yourself at him,
he'll never come.* And every time he does come by
he takes a look and says, *Nah, not this time.*
Maybe he's saving her—not for last, for of course
there is never a last. Maybe he's saving her
for that one day when he'll be sure she's the right one;
he'll drop his scythe and gather her into his arms:
white limbs, silver hair, purple nightgown
rippling in the wind.

Voyager

I.

You were like the last leaf, gone
from green to autumn red, that clung
to the vine into December, just

because it did, through sun and rain
and wind until finally a strong gust
sheared you off and you were gone.

II.

When you left this world,
you abandoned your body like a dress
tossed aside after a night of dancing.

I imagine you—a spark launched
skyward, a comet fording the dark
ocean of the universe.

You don't have to call to me, Voyager.
I will join you in my time. They say
deep peace will guide you on your journey
into the sea of everything.

III.

You used to wonder about the soul—
where it goes, what it is. You asked
a holy man once, imagining a world
without the body's needs. *I think
that's where we're headed,* his reply.
You laughed about that for years.

You liked to think the departed stay close,
watching, guiding. So when you were leaving,
I could only be happy for you:
You're going to find out all about it, Mama!

IV.

But you are gone now; I wait
to feel you near, to hear your spirit voice.

You left behind the earthly you—
your scent lingers among the clothes
I took from your closet, your old concerns
breathe among your typewritten pages
and canvases where a younger you
laid your visions down in paint.

All that's left of you now
is everything that's missing.

II.

Sacraments

Clothe Me

—After "The Beekeeper" photograph by Richard Avedon

Come to me, darlings
Nuzzle my ears
with your song
Tickle my skin
with velvet feet
Tattoo me with tales
of your many
comings-home

I give you my self
Naked and tender
Dotted with pollen

I am not fond of clothes
Dress me in what
I will never outgrow
Dress me in what
will not wear away
Make me a garment
I will never remove
A raiment more vital
than gold

For the rest of my life
Darlings, do me
one kindness please:
    From this day on
    clothe me only in bees

Sparking Joy

I miss my black shirt.
It had snaps and long sleeves.
It was soft, though made from plastic.
It was cozy when I needed cozy,
served as a jacket when I didn't.
It used to be my mother's shirt
until she gave it to me.
I wore it all the time.
It's there in the photo of me
on a visit to the farm.
I look so much better there,
my younger self smiling
beneath a tangelo tree
sky deep blue, desert hills rising
in pink pleats behind the reservoir.
I wore that black shirt
until its softness grew rough.
I gave it away when I thought
it didn't spark joy.
Now I miss that black shirt.
I don't need my clothes to spark joy.
But I need that soft black shirt with snaps
and the collar that framed my smiling
younger face.
I miss the farm.
I miss my father.
I miss my mother.
I miss my sister.
I miss my soft black shirt with snaps.

Orchid Cactus

I rise to a sky of milky stillness,
yet the plants are moving quietly

in their roots in a gentle unfurling
of leaf, a lengthening of stem.

For everything all around and in us
moves this way. Teeth emerge

from gums, nails like tiny glaciers
crawl across the nail bed, and life

pushes us along its moody current
toward an endpoint which is just

another new unfurling in a tale
of atoms moving within molecules.

Observe the squirrel who stands
and twitches her tail beneath the arm

of the cactus that is just now
preparing its wands to open

the silken flames of its flowers
to the milk-white sky.

Sacrament

To ford the river of wild mustard
we lift our knees like drum majors
marching through tangled undergrowth.
We bathe in the gold dust of it all,
the dog's black coat flecked
with pollen even after the ride home.
I think of all the microscopic
organisms we carry on and in
our bodies as we walk among the still-
flowering, now-towering plants,
welcome all of this to my hair,
to my clothes, to my lungs,
taking in the sacred body of Earth.

The Truth about Colors

He insists I get the wire frames;
my tortoise shells are so last decade.
But I have always worn tortoise shells.
They are my style! He wears me down,
talks me into transition lenses because
where I am going there will be snow
and it might hurt my eyes. But I want
to see colors as they are supposed to be,
not some off-shade! Again, he wears me
down. He can sever me from my emotions
with the sword of his logic;
they scatter and hide, but at night
while he sleeps, they whisper to me
from under the bed. *Shh,* I tell them.
Someday. Someday what?
I've given in again. When the glasses
arrive, I go for a walk alone
in a summer-dry field. The sky looks green,
the yellow grass sepia brown. At night
I glimpse the two of us in the mirror:
my new glasses are exactly like his,
wire-framed and tinted, hiding the truths
about colors, and love, and everything else.

Blue Nude

We did not spend Christmas
together that year,
my husband and I, but
before he left
for wherever he was going
with the woman
who was older,
sexier, more
accomplished than I,
he brought over
such nice gifts:
a white turtleneck
(I already had one)
and a print
of a Matisse Blue Nude.
I stayed home that day.
It was cold, gray, snowless.
And because I was in fact
relieved to have him gone,
although it hurt, although
it would take me years
to understand what we both
must have known
in the deep wordless core,
the faceless woman,
blue limbs folded in a pose
that is almost yoga,
a pose he must have seen me in
dozens of times
in our few years together,
has hung on a wall
in every home
I've lived in ever since.
The ivory background
deepening to a pale gold—
her only sign of age.

Visiting Spring

Among the skeletons
of trees I follow in spring's
shy first footsteps, see
how spring has brushed
the boughs with chilly
fingertips, pimpling them
with buds. Birds call out
but I can't name their voices.
Robins flutter among the leaves,
and tiny kinglets who won't stay
long enough for my camera
to capture their souls. Who
is the squawker in the distance?
What sound does the cardinal
make? From across the field
a blackbird raises its voice.
Though I am not from here,
though I can't make out any
of his words, that voice—
like a harmonica, an accordion—
like yours, Best Beloved,
I'd know it anywhere.

C'est Joli, Hein?

When we get to Paris we drop our bags inside the dark
hotel room and head off down Montparnasse for our first
French meal. We are 19, beautiful, brilliant, and between us

there is not one ounce of fat. In flawless college French,
we order wine because at last we can, with our *omelettes aux épinards*.
Tipsy, jet-lagged, and chic in our denim bell bottoms, we stumble

onto the nearly-empty boulevard. Parisians are either on vacation,
for it is August, or doing whatever natives do on hot summer afternoons.
But we are in Paris! Without parents! And tomorrow,

we'll head for Grenoble for a year abroad that we invented
and sold to our parents. We are invincible! But suddenly,
I hear my friend gasp; she grabs my arm and soon I see him:

baggy khakis, open raincoat, unzipped fly, dangling dong
swaying side-to-side as he approaches and says: *C'est jolie, hien*?
We scurry to our seedy hotel where we see a man in women's lingerie

giggling on the stairs. In our room, we lie in the sweltering darkness
and wait for the streets to fill up before going out again. Decades later
this becomes a story I tell ninth graders in my French classes so that

if they learn nothing more, they at least will know how to say
in French that something is pretty.

Seeing Paris

In our bathroom, ribbony damp strips
reveal a dank and rotting world
beneath an antique garden that was once
new wallpaper. *We've got to fix this*,
I tell my husband.
No, I like it this way, he says.
It reminds me of Paris.

I think of Paris today as I look at my face
in the bathroom mirror.
So many people keep their faces up
as we might our bathroom walls,
moist and pale, pulled up tight,
stitched and stapled; they even learn
to free their faces of feeling,
to meet the world with a mask
that is smooth and shiny and which may
indeed look good, but we are not fooled.
You can see death's shadow
on their gleaming hair
if you know how to look for it.

I want my own face to bear the memory
of every time I ever cried or smiled
raised my brows or frowned, every time
I screamed or felt like screaming,
every time my body convulsed with laughter,
every dream that ever darted across
my sleeping lids. I want my face
to be a panorama of experience, a book
that one might really want to read,
not some smooth slate whose past
has plainly been erased. I want this face
to seize strangers by the collar, scream
Here is my life! I have loved

this messed-up life!
I want my husband to look at my face
twenty years from now and see
something beautiful that he remembers.
I want him to look at my face
and see Paris.

Praise

Sit, I tell the dog as we reach the corner.
He looks up at me, but avoids my eyes
the way I avoid the face of the clock
when I'm running late. He doesn't want
to sit, doesn't see the point. I jerk
on the leash and he puts his bottom down.
The light changes immediately. *See?*
I tell him. *You did that! You made
the light change just by sitting down!*
I don't feel bad, lying to my dog—
he knows the difference, knows
that what matters is not what I say
but how I say it. We turn down our street,
toward the biscuit I have trained him
to expect which tells him he has done
something wonderful by simply being a dog.
I unhook the leash, he looks up:
One two three four five, I say and pat
his eager head. The biscuit is crunchy
and shaped like our mail man.
The clock on the microwave greets me
with approval. *Time well spent!* it says.
I know praise when I see it.

Fugue

Bach knits a fugue around our house
this fine autumn morning, in shades
of red, rust, earthen brown; Corelli
fills our rooms with flowers for Vivaldi
to gild, flinging his brush and spattering gold
while outside Mozart jumps up and down
on piles of fallen leaves shouting
Look at me! Look at me!

They'll keep this up forever, while we
at our breakfast table amid our papers
and our pens will one day be as gone
as the toast and coffee, gone as the leaves
that gather on the lawn, gone as the wind
that plays through the trees a doleful
variation in A.

Night Journey

Into the calm-flowing river
Morpheus dips his oar

Each dip makes a ring
that circles in moonlight
behind us

Across the water's quiet face
the belly of sleep's canoe
draws a vanishing seam

My dreams unspool
along the shadowed shore

The Stories of My Dreams

I don't even know the stories
of my own dreams;
they're more obscure to me
than the names of the trees
in these unfamiliar woods,

as unknown and unseen
as the workings of my pancreas
and spleen, as hidden
as the wildlife that moves
through the tall grass
beyond the pines. I know better

the faces of the four deer
that gathered by the fence
last evening than I know
the dreams that roamed
the brambles of last night's
sleep, for the deer stared
through my lighted window,
lifted white tails, turned
and quickly stepped away;

my dreams dispersed between
the thunder and the rain,
leaving nothing in their wake—
no crumb, no clue, not even
hoof prints cradling the dew.

The Guys Who Work Inside My Head

I don't know their names or gender
or whether they even have a gender.
I forget they're even there like I forget
a name, a fact, a necessary detail.
I only have to wonder aloud and move on
to another thought when I feel a little tap
on my shoulder or sense the presence
of a calm being behind me and there he is,
or she, or it, handing me a folder
wrapped in a metaphor containing
the datum I couldn't bring to mind
that short time ago. Then I can go on
living, assured that my mind still works,
that the guys in there have not run off
to serve a younger or more facile mind,
that they're with me still in their khakis,
buttoned-down shirts and wire-rimmed
glasses, poised to run to the file box
where they know just where to find
my username and password, the place
where we took that photo with the sea
crashing behind us, or the name
of that actor, you know, the guy
who starred in that movie with that
actress, you know, the pretty one
with the wide smile and the shining teeth.

October Afternoon

There were yellow leaves
pale sunlight

someone on the ridge
with a saxophone

a slow pensive raga
spiraling into the glen

the notes sifting down
in gold leaves at our feet.

I used to think I didn't like
the saxophone

I used to think
we would always be friends.

III.

Water Rising

Earth's Mercy

We ride Earth's back
but she doesn't buck us off.
When she shudders we feel it.
When she bucks, things fall.
We know that worse can happen,
that we are at her mercy.
But Earth has no mercy,
no desire. We are at the mercy
of life's unspooling wire;
we've no more power
than the sea has over fire.

Caveat Lepus

Rabbit pretends
not to look
but sees me,
stands so still
in the grass
watching
with round eye
beneath
the columns
of its ears.
No need to flee;
I pose no
present danger.
I look behind
to where it stands
still as granite,
watching.
I am no predator,
true. But rabbit,
oh rabbit,
you have no idea.

"Mister Lincoln"

I put my face
to the wide globe
of the rose,
to the place

where, velvet
red enrobed,
its petals
meet a chaos
of ragged silk

and fill my head
with the scent,
my heart the desire,
to be

a bee, to drunken
dance in this
fragrant room
of blooming fire

Bach Cello Suite

The cello's voice—both warm and keen
caroms off the octaves' walls.

I thought the song would carry me
to sleep; instead I lie awake

and wander the corridors of music,
trying the knobs, following the sounds

along the tightrope of each clef,
listening deep to the voices of the strings

that join the mind's imaginings
with the breath of wind through birch leaves,

the sun's shifting gaze reaching down
to the creek's bottom, leaf-strewn

and smooth as the prelude, sandy,
sun-dappled, fresh as the saraband.

Flesh Remembers

They chopped down the sycamore. I watched a man
feed the tree's weeping flesh to a grinder, flesh so red
I expected bone to poke out white, accusing.

When they pruned the pine tree, they hacked
the branches, leaving each one red on the end,
welling with sap that fell to the ground like tears.

I tripped over a stump by a campfire last summer.
The gash on my shin was a chasm bleeding black
in the dark. My flesh remembers that camping trip—

cold rushing water, nights bright with stars, redwoods
like gigantic buildings, my companion asleep
at nightfall, and me in the dark, wet flesh weeping.

To My Neighbor With the Plastic Lawn

Your plastic grass is no match
for the Bermuda grass that woke
from memory's sleep, found purchase
in the lip of soil that edged around
the plastic seam and now climbs over
what is fake and clean, and spills
dry spindles in a swell of dusty green.
Your plastic grass can't smother
all that sleeps inside the soil
but even so your plastic grass
will one day have the last
and loneliest laugh: when all of us
have gone to dust your plastic lawn
will rise in wiry strings from the sod.
triumphant and immortal as a god.

Hawk

Hawk comes hunting
sparrows and finches
that gather at the feeder.
All have fled when Death
swoops down to plant
his feathered body
on the bird-whitened fence;
storied talons grip the iron perch
where a hundred little birds
have waited their turn
at the swinging box of seed.
Hawk peers through
the window where I sit
with my coffee. Yellow
eye fierce, beak like an axe
he lifts himself into the air:
wing feathers dappled brown,
body clothed in tender down,
signature tail, a flare of rust.
I can say it now:
In Death I trust.

The Happiness of Birds

Around the lake old men
cast lines into green water;
the sun sparkling on the lake
is their catch. Coots arrive,
pumping green legs through
green water, young ones
sailing behind. I want to tell
the mothers *They hurt you*
when they enter this world;
they hurt you again as they
leave your side, but the coots
with their black velvet heads
swim calmly across the channel.
They have no use for happiness.

Empty Place

How did I not notice
the water rising?
It sloshes around my ankles
when I walk; I feel it
climbing toward my knees,
pulling me back to my empty place.
She is gone now
like a balloon into the ether
and I'm left here
a crumpled pile
of hand-me-down genes.

Quarantine Spring

Death has made me
travel among strangers,
trying to stay distant,
faces stark with danger.

Home now from the funeral
I take my morning walk:
a rabbit leaps into the brush;
a squirrel scurries across
the grass and I feel a bomb
ticking in my belly.

Lilies prepare to bloom,
raise green spears to the sky.
Here I am, I tell the world.
Do as you must. My hands
have never been so clean.

Sunset in the Time of Plague

Like the Sacred Heart of Dali's Jesus
throbbing for the love of man, today's last rays
glow red within the tallest stack of vapor

Rain falls in a gray sheaf to the sea
and all around the budding world prepares,
unafraid, for night. I return to my home,

wash hands with hope, shelter this fearful,
tender body, still filled with that sunset,
that cloud, that painting—

Jesus's heart throbbing in his sacred chest, full
with love for man, even as the earth turns away
and darkness lays its heavy comfort on the land.

Fire Sky

The last May rain sent up new shoots
among the sagging spring flowers;
they all turned to kindling by September.
Now we wander through days of brown sky
and ash settling on dusty ground, air
so dark with smoke we can't see
the sun when it sets. The eerie calls
of owls color the air, their shadowy forms
thicken on tree limbs, exhausted from hunting
through the red night of afternoon.

The Wood Duck's Home

Let me live alone
in the wood duck's home
in a box on a post
at the edge of a stream.
I'll watch small fish teem
and leaves drift by
from a hole as round
as the wood duck's eye.

From here in May
I will see frogs grow,
hear cedars squeak
on the winds of spring.
The wood duck will know
to leave me alone
in the little box house
at the edge of the stream.

I'll watch sunlight widen
and yellow leaves drop
and stream water thicken
to ice and stop. And then
when the woods go quiet
with snow, I will hear
you calling and maybe then
I'll go.

Bereavement

The way the jacaranda leans away from the eave
reminds me you are gone forever. Four limbs rise

from the vee, but there's a flat place,
a plain face, where a limb has been removed.

All around that stump sprout small burly scars
with feathery fronds; somewhere in this tree

there is a need to grow a limb back in the spot
where it will never be allowed to grow; new leaves

sprout there as if to replace that one branch
that has been removed and is never coming back.

Cistern

A concrete shaft
stands at the edge
of the reservoir
by the house
that is no more.
I used to climb
the rebar rungs, peer
into the pool below,
throw a stone to hear
the resonant splash,
and shout to feel it
echo in my head.
There my face floated,
a specter on the water's
deep canvas. Sometimes
the cistern filled,
water tumbling in
from the canal.
I am that cistern now,
grief the still pool
always at the bottom,
grief the rough cascade
that rushes in.

To a Grieving Friend

When Grief with its dark bulk
bars your friend's door,
there are no right words.

In time, Grief will lie down,
close one eye and then the other.

That is when you will hear
my heart, dear friend, drumming
low and steady just outside.

Mistaken Identity

I. The Voice of Wild Yarrow

With sunset near, my mind is on the light
and not the growing things releasing scent
to the evening world. I round a corner;
the yarrow calls out:

We're here! in a voice I've never heard before.

Sometimes one instrument in the symphony
will suddenly reveal itself: the oboe raises its voice
above the strings and then the oboe is all
that you can hear. So the yarrow beckons

and I move into the crowd of it. They rise
above me, form a cove for me to stand in.
They gather 'round, nod their heavy heads
toward mine. I bathe in the music of their scent

and hear the whole world speak to me.
I thank the yarrow, go on my way,
their choir song swirling in my head,
their voices the scent of sweet dusty hay.

II. Poison-Hemlock

Last spring they beckoned me with dusty scent,
these gangly beings holding high their clusters
of tiny white flowers.

Like a crowd of sisters, they welcomed me
to stand among them. How lucky I felt
as they encircled me. I bore no prejudice,
no fear. In ignorance, I called them wild yarrow.
Should they grow so tall again this dry

and dusty year, and call me to them
with their perilous charms, newly wise, I'll yet
accept their invitation, feel honored
as I did in school when the bad girls
widened their circle, making room for me.

Moon Bathing

I.

My mother showed them to me:
tiny moons blooming at the base
of each fingernail. I would lie
in bed then, counting my moons.
This morning the remains
of last night's near full moon
balances on a cluster of palms
at the edge of the sky, its crown
the same pale white as the moon
at the base of my thumb.

II.

Last night the moon glowed
waxy-white; it lit my path
from the gate to my door
and I thought: This is *bathing*;
the full moon *bathes* the sky
in milky light. Sometimes I want
to slip outside naked and bathe
in moonlight the way I did as a girl
but now I have neighbors.

III.

Mornings when I see the moon
still in the sky after I've spent hours
dreaming and forgetting, it's like
seeing my mother again, her head
tilted fondly, her half smile asking
Did you sleep well, honey?
and I tell her *Yes, Mother, I did.*

Tamara Madison grew up near the fault line in the California desert. Her poems have appeared in *Chiron Review*, the *Worcester Review*, *A Year of Being Here*, and many other print and online journals. Several of her poems have been featured on the Writers Almanac and the Lyric Life. She is the author the full-length poetry collections, *Wild Domestic* and *Moraine*, and the chapbook *The Belly Remembers*, all published by Pearl Editions. *Along The Fault* was published by Picture Show Press in 2022. Read more about her at tamaramadisonpoetry.com.

www.ingramcontent.com/pod-product-compliance
Lightning Source LLC
Chambersburg PA
CBHW060350130626
46553CB00003B/1166